i want a poem
valerie senyk

Vocamus Press
Guelph, Ontario

Written by Valerie Senyk
Some rights reserved

ISBN 13: 978-0-9881049-9-0 (pbk)
ISBN 13: 978-1-928171-00-3 (ebk)

VP

Vocamus Press
130 Dublin Street, North
Guelph, Ontario, Canada
N1H 4N4

www.vocamus.net

2014

Dedication

I lovingly dedicate this work to my three fine, creative sons – Mishkin, Alexei and Callam – whose lives are poetry.

Acknowledgements

I am grateful to my husband Rob O'Flanagan for his never-failing encouragement of all my artistic endeavours and for providing me with the photograph for the cover. Our son, Callam Rodya, played with the image, designed the title, and made suggestions on the fonts. Merci, sweetie! Thanks are also due to my friend Ravi Butalia who gave me priceless feedback on the manuscript. Lastly, I gratefully acknowledge the enthusiasm, editing prowess and services of Jeremy Luke Hill of Vocamus Press.

Preface

This series began as an online conversation on what constitutes poetry. I read with great interest what oppinions the other writers, scattered throughout cyberspace, held. It brought to mind a theatre professor talking about the "crystallized language" of poetry – the idea that poetry uses very selective words. The conversation also made me reflect upon poetry that has moved me over the years, like that of Rainer Maria Rilke and Rumi, W.B. Yeats and Cohen. What did I want from poetry? I wrote a response to the online discussion in poetic form, and thus the first "I want a poem" came into being, followed by another, and another, while other writers took up the theme. Although it started as an accidental series, it has helped me to write in a more immediate way, to trust my own stream of consciousness and unconsciousness, and to realize the pleasure of mixing together image, metaphor, and sound.

i want a poem
valerie senyk

gerard manley poem

i want a poem like pomegranates
to splash my mouth

to slake my forever thirst
length of my tongue

talk to me with taste
bitter lemons to hop the ivories
of my teeth

craving that
juiced-up God-poet

gerard manley hopkins
r.i.p.

rodent poem

i want a poem to jump up
off the page
and bite me in the face

a perverse rat
of a poem

its characters
alive and hungry
for my nerve endings

pause poem

i want a poem like a comma
where breath enters a line

a floating entrance
something gentling

i could meet you
in that space

we would find the grace
of pause holding us

in a mystery of silence
before pressing onward

food poem

i want a poem all crisp fried noodles
sesame oiled bite sized greens
fragrant chicken topped with
oozing tamari and sesame seeds

i want a poem to stop hunger
and start feeding:
stop and start being two different verbs

i want to be a poem myself
drift right up to God's banquet table:

"i offer You my honey-tarted shrimp
plump Your cheeks braised coconut

just tell me Your secret for
the hungry ones"

Arizona poem

i want a poem like
a blue Arizona pool
where a dove and an olive tree
converse as ancient friends

where high clouds crisscross
with beaming jet streams
all sensations dipping into
the deep pool at my feet

pewter-stained deserts
streak by the freeways
cacti like punctuation marks
sculpt the hills

the dawn light
seeping into my room
is the colour of the heavy lemons
hanging in trees

my eyes and ears fill
with aqueous echoes
and the air I breath
is lapis blue

– for Warren

memory poem

i want a poem to kiss me
deep inside
the pearly silver shell
of soul

erase my nightmares
turn them into
delinquent good deeds

a poem to remember
who i am
when i am

and you too

needy poem

i want a poem that needs me
to write it –
says, girl, it's that stuff you form
inside your mouth and breathe
into notebooks
that i resonate with:

round soupy vowels
carefully wrapped by
candy-hard consonants
carrying all slippy-sloppy
your cheeky notions

i want a poem that
claims me for its author
makes it known: this
is the one i was looking for!
i want to be chosen by a poem

like Pirandello's
six characters beseeching him to
author their lives
and he did

today i saw
the foreign mountains far to the west
delicate ink drawings;
is there a poem that will find me
or want translating?

laborious poem

i want a poem that makes me work
sweating and grunting

like digging potatoes
in parched prairie earth

or exhuming a corpse
from my dream world

– euh
cement from toes

foreign poem

i want a poem
that shouts in a tongue
other than i speak

light and dark poem

i want a poem like
a raw star
a wound in black

moon icy and pure
in a pure ink wash

i lift my face
let sky rest on my eyes
dark cold comfort

stars making sweetness with
sugar-lights

i want a poem from this circle:
light by dark
by light and dark again

peace poem

i want a poem to stop war –

just stop it in its tracks before
the tempers and testosterone escalate
and fill the skies
with sepia stained smoke.

– this is naïve.

i would stand between two
opposing forces as they advance
wrapped in neutral white
and stop their weapons
even if i am killed.

– that too is naïve.

i sit at a desk in a little house
in a calm Canadian city
somberly aware of erupting conflicts
far away

knowing this pen will never ever
evereverever have
the power of a sword.

stormy poem

i want a poem to come at me
like a 90 kilometer wind
grab breath from my mouth
play my arms like
thrashing tree branches
buckle the stems of my legs

to be toppled
bowed low

to inhale
earth's best odor

be found sightless
like Lear
in the eye of a storm
where an epiphany waits
to penetrate

China poem

i want a poem to come
from Beijing
with muted history and traffic jams

in Mandarin
to confound me
even as it lulls

i want a poem to find me out
on the other side of the world
where i've tunnelled a hole
to escape:

North Americana normalism
arrogantism
materialism

my selfism

aggressive poem

i want a poem that launches
a velvet-gloved fist

into the other woman's face
her tight smile
her downcast eyes

splinter the breastbone that carries
my man's image like a trophy

make her crocodile tears fly

and she'll know
she'll know

this frisson of aggression
is enough:
I have folded her
in my embrace
murmured: everything's okay
it's okay

but a poet
like me
wants

stone poem

i want a poem
like a smooth river stone
to clutch in my palm
place under my pillow

while I sleep
it harvests
a multitude of voices
visitation of spirits
absorbs
the juddering earth
always always
beyond sense

i want to dream on these
to be aware

Rilke poem

i want a poem that brings back my dead
because since they died i've known
what i wanted to say to them

must catch the moment

like wind whips up a leaf
carries it a few meters until
it's dropped again: that short

(a fallen leaf is dead too)

i want a poem to entice my dead
speak to me in lavish
lavender and ice tongues

even better
give me white and lilac syllables
for my living

painless poem

I want a poem
that doesn't ache
like a swollen tooth
like birth pangs

but that's impossible
I believe that's impossible

maybe one day

God poem

i want a poem to feed an addiction
to all things beautiful and unreachable
to all things unnameable
to wanting God in me

why is He so far from anything
i might imagine?
is He too ugly to make an appearance?

ah, of course: the Blessed Beauty, the
Blessed Beauty...

and me in me

bicycle poem

i want a poem like an 8-speed pony
to cycle me about the thoroughfares
of ancient Beijing

dash between
lurching taxicabs
buses
vw's
renaults
all drunken chrome and gas-spewing

bear me down first ring Forbidden City
beneath twelve or sixteen gateways
bring me to a halt before
the last emperor's
vast and pitiful tourist site
where i dismount

kow-tow to
the wasteful gravity of history

remnant poem

i want a poem like the building
ablaze with sun outside my window
with precise historic turrets
crackle-cream facade and deep hedges

like last september's walk
following red-needled paths
their umbrella of blackened tree limbs

like the memory of our lad
laughing at his rabbit's mating antics;

your voice across telephone wires

a poem that takes my last breath
my falling dust

away

night poem

i want a poem to sing me
when stuck against my
dark pillow fretting

sing sing
like a summer's storm

i want a poem to tuck me
into bed on time
but blaze my trails
out of time

picture poem

i want a poem so beautiful
it will drench my eyes

princely
comely
powder white
safflower lipped

a poem to swoon by
reaching out a hand to touch

can't touch:
do they make them like that?

and this poem will have
a moving mountain for a soul

playground poem

i want a poem that tips me up
like a teeter totter

brings me down hard
crash
bump

a muscle in sheep's clothing
the wolf slain

black hole poem

i want a poem that
keeps you from your darkness

that stops you from falling back
into that soft black hole
you've turned to since boyhood
it's too comfortable for you

you know it well:
the night of the soul
the noisy vortex
whirling everyone inside

i don't do well in darkness
never did

can I make you a poem that brings you
a cup of light? to sip like tea?
to splash on your face?
to dip your tired fingers?

to annoint your entire self

and reveal that knight in shining laughter
who saves rather than buries?

blind poem

i want a poem that will blind me
force me to grope toward

dusty mountain peaks beyond sunsets
desert beyond footprints
coconuts that drip their milk

past wind-driven cliffs Antarctica

my homeland somewhere
every where

message poem

i want a poem painted
as a black square

i'll slick it over with white gesso
viscous and thick
and while it's still wet
dig into it with
sharpened objects
making little runes
and large scratchy gestures
– the delicate and the grotesque –
to peek through to
the hard black surface beneath

this is my speech to you
this is my letter
what does it say?

it says: you left
you went into the black
became white
and i search for you

love poem

i want a poem to bite
hard
within its kiss

kiddie poem

i want a poem i want a poem
baby-play
mother's milk
(and all that)

kite-coloured pictures
to gnaw with teething gums

words & letters
like hardtack biscuits
honeyed nipples

now

snow poem

I want a poem like
a silent snowfall outside a small window

its silence weighty like God
soft as dim memory

a white drifting out there
while I am in here

looking

a lost and found flake

restless poem

i want a poem like a restless soul
to solve this thorny problem:
what to do?

park one's sorry ass
on a barstool?
turn to stargazing drenched in
the light of the full moon?
drive the car into a rockface
on a northern highway turn-off?

there have to be
other options.

okay girl –
run run run
runrunrunrunrunrunrunrun

the moon's glaze will turn you into
speeding white air

feline poem

i want a stretching poem
e-l-o-n-g-a-t-e-d
sleek with shiny fur
toes ecstatically splayed
mouth all grin

i'll play my hands along that spine
define the ripple of muscle and sinew
from collar
to the end of a tail

repeat the motion

repeat the motion

purring

changing poem

i want a poem
that changes my life

i want to change my life

to turn like a top
and when i stop
all will be disarranged

disgorged
disarmed
disbanded

you may see me still
but inside i spin

pilgrim poem

i want a poem folded in my palm
like a handkerchief
saturated with the scent of rose

to recall a threshold strewn
with red and pink blossoms
beyond which there is no passing

forehead pressed upon petals
eyes turned to an inward light
whose gold burnishes my sight

i would become a pilgrim
with her nose dipped in cupped hands
offering it all up

take me up

space poem

i want a poem that will never rhyme
no matter how hard i try
that will find me
a bit of space to breathe

man it's hard to breathe in Beijing
but even harder in Canada
because the pressures are
so huge

you don't see them until you're in
the midst of a million bicycles

singing poem

i want a poem that will sing
a dark and hopeful anthem
asking for a miracle

i want a poem that will deliver me a baby
like the one forever appearing
in my dreams
though she is always lost
or taken

maybe i already have
the poem i want
sometimes i sing to myself
my voice quaking
with grief or silly joy

maybe i poem a want

empty poem

i want a poem like,
okay,
a brand-new lined notebook
empty with promise

where the alphabet imagines herself
into gorgeous syllables and sounds

pen hovering
dripping India ink
not yet touching the page

the question
the anticipation

i wear lettered beads on a wrist
an anklet of bells
that ching where i walk

maybe
silence is
never empty

ugly poem

i want a poem that shows
every crack and crevasse in my heart

like the two deep ugly ones:
one of my making, the other his

the humid scent of blood
will seep through the words
like scratch'n sniff

i will hold this poem open to those
who tell me i am beautiful
so they see all

and when my body starts to crack
the fissures deepen
the bones dislodge
and cells spill like pomegranate seeds

the poem will be complete

flood poem

i want a poem flooding me
with debris and foam
and power i cannot fight
to wash over me and the world
to sweep us all out to sea
to sea
seas-on us
excoriate the barnacles of living

clear the stench from the air
release the broken glass from my belly

let the watery verses come
let them refresh
let my end-of-world-dreams come true

it's time

Photo by Crystal Bueckert

About the Author

Valerie Senyk was born to first generation Canadians in Winnipeg in the midst of a flood, one of six children. At the age of nine, she knew she would be an artist, and she published her first poem at age eleven under an assumed name. At seventeen she embraced the Baha'i Faith, and she has allowed it to inspire and teach her, giving her the courage to live life as an ongoing adventure for learning.

She has followed an eclectic and interdisciplinary path as an artist. She received a BFA in Fine Arts and an MA in Drama from the University of Saskatchewan, in Saskatoon, and she taught Theatre Arts at universities in both Saskatchewan and Ontario for twenty-three years. She has worked as an actor, director, and is a published and recorded performance poet. She has experimented with documentary and alternative filmmaking, and has recently returned to her roots as a visual artist. She writes book reviews for the *Kitchener Record* and a faith column for the *Guelph Mercury*.

Senyk currently lives in Guelph with her husband Rob O'Flanagan.

www.ingramcontent.com/pod-product-compliance
Lightning Source LLC
Chambersburg PA
CBHW020023050426
42450CB00005B/621